LOVE IS AN ACTION WORD

LOVE IS AN ACTION WORD

A BACK-TO-BASICS RELATIONSHIP GUIDE FOR HUSBANDS AND WIVES

KURT BROADNAX

J. Merrill
PUBLISHING

J Merrill Publishing, Inc., Columbus 43207
www.JMerrill.pub

Library of Congress Control Number: 2021906954
ISBN-13: 978-1-950719-98-3 (Paperback)
ISBN-13: 978-1-950719-97-6 (eBook)

Title: Love Is An Action Word
Author: Kurt Broadnax
Editing: Dennis Brown

CONTENTS

FOREWORD

We live in a nation where the family structure is decaying.

In previous generations, most people in the United States were raised with an awareness of moral values, knowing the difference between right and wrong.

During the last 50 years, much has changed. We have now reached a place where what was once taught as right is being defined as wrong and what was once clearly wrong is no said to be right.

The heart of the problem is the broken and dysfunctional family. Since the mid-1960s, an increasing number of children have been growing up in single-parent homes. I know. I was one of them, and I know many others who have had the same experience or were raised by grandparents or other relatives.

Thankfully, many single-parent families have raised their children well. But we are reminded almost every day by the growing crime rate among our teens and now pre-teens that families are broken, parents are absent from the home, or simply have lost their moral bearings. Children are having babies when they have never even learned to take care of themselves.

Our children's moral fiber is being corrupted by the growing exposure to pornography in magazines, movies, and the internet. An increase in prostitution is a glaring issue in nearly every city, creating a community where decency and commitment are becoming rare. Child abuse in the home is increasing at an alarming rate, reflecting only the reported cases.

The family structure is often so broken that our children are growing up broken themselves. Not only does the home need both parents, but if those parents are not morally and spiritually healthy, the kind of issues discussed above will only become worse. Parents need to be morally and spiritually healthy even before children are a part of the picture.

The focus of this book is the relationships between men and women who choose to create a life and family together. Life together needs to create an atmosphere in which husbands and wives are mutually committed to nurturing and caring for each other. If children are to grow into healthy adults and have lasting, loving relationships, they need to see stability replacing the all-too-common images of divorce and instability.

The message in our day is that divorce is normal, even expected. People routinely and casually drop one partner and pick up another. That message is plastered all over television, movies, and the internet, and sadly, we mindlessly support their twisted values.

Stable relationships let our children, neighbors, and friends discover a better way. Those couples who are making their marriages work are passing on to others the value of commitment that builds a strong relationship.

Yet, we are merely human beings with all our best intentions, flawed and prone to imperfect results. And so, in the end, we must acknowledge that God alone can guide us and shape us together to reflect His plan for us as couples and families. His desire is for us to shine with His grace in a world that seems intent on destroying the basic foundation of our homes. When we allow Him to be at the center of every relationship, He will hold the relationship together.

BASIC TRAINING

In my younger days, I enlisted in the Army.

That experience taught me a simple truth: as a soldier, if I were to function as the Army intends and with the many tasks they assign, I first had to learn "the basics." Everything about a soldier's life is built or extends from the Seven Core Army Values:

- **Duty**
- **Loyalty**
- **Respect**
- **Selfless service**
- **Honor**
- **Integrity**
- **Personal courage**

These values and qualities form a foundation for

life in general. Everything we do in life should reflect our commitment to these principles.

And that is very much the case with building healthy, productive, and lasting relationships. But it is especially true with the relationship between a man and a woman who want to form a life together. Life together survives and thrives when the basics of a relationship are in place and carefully guarded.

People know how to get into relationships. However, they often do not know when *not* to get into one, and it is clear that many do not know how to maintain a relationship when they have one.

The most significant reason for the breakdown of the home is the breakdown of the relationship of the husband and the wife. People learn to live in relationships from their own home lives, but homes with parents who fail to build their relationships on loving values fail to provide the basic training their children need to be modeled for them.

The point here is that we cannot hope to fix the home unless we repair the relationship models in the home.

Even if they have no children, the relationship between a man and a woman still serves as a model to others. If the basics of a loving, healthy relationship are missing or ignored, that relationship is toxic to the rest of the family and everyone else around them.

Let's look for a moment at the basics of a lasting

and loving relationship. Healthy relationships are built on mutual commitments to:

1. **Value each other**
2. **Nurture each other**
3. **Know each other**
4. **Build up each other**

These are the basic building blocks for relationships, and while they may overlap with each other, each is distinctive and needs to be mentioned separately.

Loving is more than an emotional connection and certainly much more than a physical one. The bond between a man and a woman, who choose to build a life of love with each other, must include a firm sense of esteem and value for one another. In the end, love is a choice to commit to the care and growth of another.

A commitment to value, nurture, genuinely know, and build up each other cannot happen, however, without a sense of obligation (i.e., duty) to maintain loyalty, respect, selflessness, honor, integrity, and courage as the values that underlie every part of life in a relationship.

WHERE TO BEGIN

*T*he focus was on basics in the introduction, so let's start with a simple basic fact.

Whether you are going on a vacation or to the grocery store, you have to start somewhere. Every time there is an ending point, there has to be a starting point. If that sounds too basic, think again.

Every loving and healthy relationship needs a starting point.

That starting point is knowing who you are and having a strong sense of your true value as a human being. If you truly have a clear and healthy sense of who you are, you will be able to enjoy a healthy relationship in your life.

You may have heard that you should love others as you love yourself (Jesus of Nazareth, Matthew 22:39). If you understand who you are and value yourself, you will be capable of valuing and nurturing someone else. Those who neglect a spouse or family genuinely suffer from a damaged sense of self-value and, unfortunately, treats others the way they treat themselves.

A failure to have a genuine sense of self-respect and a sense of your worth will hinder the new relationship from being the beautiful experience you want it to be.

So, what did Jesus mean when He spoke about loving yourself?

His words in Matthew 22:39 follow an even more fundamental truth. Jesus was responding to a question about what the greatest commandment was, and His answer had two parts:

> *"You must love the Lord your God with all your heart, all your soul, and all your mind." This is the first and greatest commandment. A second is equally important: "Love your neighbor as yourself"*

His response tells us two things: loving others is directly related, even dependent on loving ourselves, but this is second to loving God with all that is within us.

Jesus is summarizing the Ten Commandments given in Exodus 20. The first four of those commandments speak about our relationship with God. The last six talk about how He wants us to relate to others.

Note what He says about this "second commandment:" loving others is as important as loving God. Both parts of His answer are of equal importance. But how can that be? Isn't our relationship with God more important than anything else? The answer is "yes," but to understand the Commandments, we have to look at more than Exodus 20.

Remember that in Exodus 19, God is establishing a covenant relationship with Israel. This relationship is an agreement or contract between Him and His people. God wanted them to live among the pagan nations in a way that reflected Him and allowed those nations to see how different life would be under His loving authority compared to their relationships with the many false gods they followed.

That difference was on display by the trusting relationship Israel had with God on the one hand and how that allegiance to Him defined how they treated others who were part of this convenient relationship.

I can tell you on the Bible's authority that we must have a relationship with God to have healthy and loving relationships with each other. We simply cannot fully have the second without the first. But

God Himself defined both of these as equally important because they are both a part of the same redemptive relationship.

Our relationship with others reflects our relationship with Him. We have to respond to His offer for us to live in a relationship with Him, and the moment we do that, we are made capable by His grace to live in the kind of relationship with others that reflects His relationship with us.

The bottom line here is that these two factors of our lives are not separate. One cannot exist with the other. Those who don't love others don't love God, and those who claim to love God do not act lovingly toward others do not truly love Him.

Notice that the four building blocks of a relationship listed in the Introduction apply to both our love relationship with God and our loving relationship with others.

Both need to be based on a deep sense of value toward the one we love.

Those who value the love of a holy God will, in turn, love others because God loves them.

Those who nurture their relationship with God through prayer and reflection, with time in His Word and lovingly serving Him, will also need to nurture their relationship with others and become servants to them, just as Jesus took on the role of a servant in His earthly life.

Those who are in daily communion with God

allow God to reveal Himself to them in their spirit. The hunger and thirst to have Him reveal Himself more and more to them. Those then are equipped to grow in their relationship with others, know them, and recognize their changes and growth.

And those who are built up by God's love, enabling them to become more like Him, will have to Godly motivation to invest energy and time in others to help them become stronger and grow to know God more clearly as well.

God initiates our covenant life with Him. Our starting point is our response to His invitation to live the covenant life. When we respond, we embrace one commitment that has two goals: loving Him and loving others to reflect our covenant life.

The relationship with God builds a foundation within us by His grace on which you and I must build our journey of a loving relationship. That relationship then extends His grace to others. His presence in our lives is the glue that holds our relationship with each other together.

If one mate is walking in a loving relationship with God and the other is not, the hope that the other mate will someday come to experience His love is anchored in the Christian mate's consistent example of grace extended to the other. Imperfectly as that may be, the soil of grace still bears the presence of God in the heart of the other.

LOVE HAS NO COLOR

Since we know that love has its origin and fullness in God Himself, we also know that He is also our final authority on the nature of love. In His covenant of love with us, He invites us to love Him fully. That love then is reflected in the way we live with others around us so that they discover what living and loving God is like.

When we understand that God is love and loves us all unconditionally, we realize that He intends for us to have loving relationships. There is no barrier to the love that is centered in God.

As accurate as that is about relationships in general, it should be even more so when talking about life with a mate. The media reinforces the racial division that makes everything about the color of your skin.

But those who live in a loving relationship with

God should be the first to set aside the color barrier. It's time we listen to the challenge to make the content of character more critical than the color of someone's skin.

The world we live in has become more accepting of people getting married outside of their race. Yet those who do still have to be prepared to deal with the social objections of many. But there will always be challenges in a relationship in which couples are trying to blend different cultural or social worlds. And a couple must not forget that the children face the same kind of adjustments and pressures from their peers.

How can we continue to allow the media and the culture of hate to tell us who we can or cannot develop relationships with? Society may look at how you dress, the way you speak, and your general appearance. Yet even if our differences are social or cultural, love builds bridges, not barriers.

We can be treated differently because of how we dress or speak, even from our general impressions. But we must not let this spirit invade our minds.

If a man and a woman from different social or racial backgrounds want to build a life together, they should take care to be conscious of their differences and value them. But there is nothing in the example of God's covenant love that suggests that any social distinction is a barrier to love.

1 Samuel 16:17 makes it clear that while our

human eyes look at outward appearances, God looks at the heart. God sees us and knows us not by the color of our skin but by the content of the heart.

If you spend time with God in prayer and Bible study, you will learn to see others through His eyes and connect with them heart to heart.

Let me say here that there aren't any perfect people in this world. We all have some shortcomings and even failures. You will not be an ideal mate any more than the one you marry. As we will discuss in later chapters, we need mutual nurturing, hearts of forgiveness, and time together to build each other up.

And a life of mutual love, respect, nurturing, and growing, has no color.

KEEPING LOVE ALIVE

*L*ove in its purest form is spiritual.

The world has invented its sources on which they claim we can build relationships. They tell us that we can look to the horoscope or tarot cards or Eastern mysticism. They present us with talk shows and self-help books that claim to have the secrets we can use to find and maintain love.

The culture of our society has redefined love to be emotional and physical and has designed path after path for us to follow that may feel good to our human senses but leads us away from the true Source of love.

Love's origins are holy, and our love for each other can only be real when God's love is active within us.

Keeping love alive in your relationship with your

husband or wife can become a somewhat confusing subject if you listen only to worldly wisdom. But it is not that mysterious when you remember the true Source of love. Talk about God's place in your lives. Read His word together and pray together. The old saying "The family that prays together stays together" is as true now as it ever was.

Be quick to apologize and ask forgiveness from each other when you have not reflected God's grace in your relationship. And together, rededicate your relationship with God as well.

But there are some things that you need to guard carefully.

Let me mention a problem that confronts many couples today. Frequently, spouses drag their experiences from previous relationships into their new ones. Old failures and old feelings that are carried over infect the current relationship. He supposes that she is as unfeeling as a previous woman in his life. She expects that he will be as distant as another once was. And both may have trust issues that came earlier in their lives.

Part of knowing your spouse is deciding to let grace define him or her. Each relationship will have its own hiccups and hurdles, but to impose previous assumptions on the current relationship will push grace aside.

This is true whether the assumptions are good or bad. A strength in one relationship may not look the same in another. People show their love in different ways. The way they respond to each other may not be what you were used to in a previous relationship. Be a careful observer who gets to know the strengths and weaknesses of your current relationship.

Work with what *is*, not what *was*.

A significant area of conflict can often be the workplace. If one is working outside of the home and the other is caring full time for the family, the workplace can interfere with both. When husbands and wives, dads and moms both have jobs, both may become consumed by their work, and the relationship may suffer.

Be careful that you do not look at your job or career as the way to define who you are and how much you are worth. You may tend to invest extra time and energy to perform with excellence and impress your boss. Some have visions of climbing the corporate ladder to achieve greater success. But you are more than what the job says you are.

Now let me be clear, all of those things may be reasonable goals, but they may throw your relationship with your spouse out of line. These things must never be allowed to be the first place in your life. The job must never overshadow your family life after you clock out and go home. The frustrations nor the achievements on the job should dominate your thoughts or conversations at home.

You can discuss your day briefly, then turn your attention to those around you and what they need at that moment.

The task that ultimately defines you and your worth is the care of the relationship you have forged with your family. This is the gift with which God's grace has entrusted you.

Take notice, especially of the parts of your working day that were hard and perhaps made you uncomfortable or angry. Take as much time as you need before you go into the house to get your attitude in check. Leave the trouble from work at the door or in your car. Do not transfer your negative feelings to your spouse or children, but go into the house with a positive attitude. Your spouse needs your care, not your problems. He or she has had enough problems of their own that day.

The exception to that "rule" is when the problem at home during the day relates to your children. When correction is needed, parents need to be on the same page. If a child is facing some difficulty at school or in the neighborhood, care must be given to make him or her stronger and at the same time provide a sense of reinforcement for the spouse that may have already had to deal with the matter. Remember, your relationships in the home need the same four strategies that any relationship needs.

Leaving your workplace issues behind can free you to invest yourself in the task of passing on the values you want your family to embrace. Whether the family is just you and a spouse, or if it includes children or even other family members, your job is to live in a way that all of them see in you the kind of values they need to be healthy and strong in their lives.

Children, in particular, learn to love and commit to their future relationships by the examples they see from their parents. They need to see mom and dad hugging each other, being tender with each other, and hearing them say "I love you" to each other often. They learn to nurture others when they have experienced nurturing relationships themselves. They need to see how their parents handle mistakes with each other, including apologies and how relationships are restored.

Take time to reflect on how you handle your job frustrations and not let them damage your children or your spouse. Family life cannot always be about how needy you are; instead, life together must always focus on how much the family needs your care. Imposing your needs on the family can cause the children or our spouse to fail to realize how much God values them.

If your workplace struggles are allowed to infect your home life, you may find yourself reacting unkindly to your family. Homes have been destroyed by the anger from the workplace being taken out on the family. If this escalates, children and spouses can become subjects of emotional abuse or worse.

To keep your love alive and growing, you must also be aware of each other's emotional needs. Just as you provide food and shelter, providing emotional support is necessary to nurture each other.

Life is full of struggles and challenges. Each spouse will inevitably experience times of disappointments, failures, physical changes, and social shifts. Each needs the other to be supportive and encouraging. Each requires a listening ear and a helping hand to care for the routines of life when these struggles interfere. Tending to each other's emotional health is every bit as important as responding to physical needs.

Families experience emotional challenges when life's changes take place. Babies come, and with them are sleepless nights and weary days. Each spouse needs to be a part of the adjustment time.

Children grow through stages of rebellion or social awkwardness, for example. They may be affected by bullying at school or in the neighborhood. They can develop learning difficulties that affect their self-image. Whatever the challenge may be, parents must not let the matter rest too heavily with one or the other.

Coping with family challenges effectively requires us to know the strengths and weaknesses of our spouses. We need to understand where and how our spouses were raised and their relationships as they grew up.

Tough times will come. Deaths in the family, loss of a job, a loss of trust, and a sense of safety can change the course of our lives. And in today's world, such unthinkable events like adultery, abuse, betrayal sexual violence is all too common. Families need well-developed communication skills. Spouses need strong sensitivity to recognize the signs of stress and trauma that cause changes in behavior. And most of all, each must wrap the other in grace and fresh strength, acceptance, and affirmation.

Such struggles can be more effectively met by wisdom and patience. Make sure you let your spouse know in as many ways as possible that your love has not changed, that he or she is still the treasure of your life.

Take time to discuss relationship problems. Choose a time and a place when you can be alone with your spouse. Anytime such talks take place while emotions are high, it will not go well. Each of you needs to be confident that your thoughts or fears can be heard without being judged.

Whether in these planned times or any other time, never dwell on negative issues for a long time. Speak gently, and change the subject if the issue can't be resolved right then. Later, when the time is right, and the emotions have cooled, address such issues with understanding. And seek common ground for the best possible win-win outcome.

Spouses must live together with integrity. If you promise something, then keep your word. When you are apart, each spouse needs to know where the other is in case of emergencies. If one spouse has to travel on business, they should make a phone call at least once a day to the other spouse, letting him or her know that you care about what is going on at home. Do not neglect time to nurture your spouse emotionally, physically, and spiritually.

KEEPING YOUR LOVE
STRONG

NURTURING – LOVING AND CARING PHYSICALLY

*S*omeone has said that a relationship that lasts grows strong. But *longer* doesn't always mean *stronger*. Even an unhealthy relationship can last a long time.

There are two truths about the relationship that grows stronger over time. First, only a healthy relationship grows strong; and secondly, strength is produced by nurturing.

Nurturing someone only happens when someone makes a choice. The nurturer chooses to cultivate the life of another, to invest time and energy to encourage and nourish someone in a way that allows that person to grow and flourish.

Three areas of one's life that need to be nurtured:

- Physical
- Emotional

- Spiritual

Let's begin with physical nurturing.

Despite society's distorted image of the relationship of a husband and wife, the physical need is not all about sex. A nurturing relationship is primarily about providing a home where you and your spouse are safe and healthy.

The home is not about the real estate but the relationship. Circumstances may not always allow you to live in the largest or best-looking house on the block, but wherever you live can be a safe and comfortable environment. Both the husband and the wife may hope to live in a better house or a different neighborhood eventually. Yet, each can feel the loving care of the other and share the desire for their home to be a welcoming place where everyone in the home does not feel threatened or unwanted.

The furniture may be used, but the place can be clean. And the safety of open arms at the door is far more important than physical or material luxuries. A nurturing home is filled with the security of respect and affirmation of each other's values. A nurturing spouse communicates in every way possible that the other is the priority.

Nurturing each other requires you to nurture yourself. The Biblical directive to love others as you love yourself is pretty straightforward. If you do not take care of yourself or neglect proper care for yourself, how can your spouse assume you will take care of him or her.

Both spouses should take care of themselves physically. How you care for yourself sets a standard for others in the family. Staying physically fit, avoiding unhealthy eating habits, cleanliness, and grooming help avoid health issues while at the same time telling your spouse that you want to be around to take care of them.

And self-respect is contagious.

Nurturing each other physically naturally involves times of intimacy. Since the cultural slant on sex today is more self-focused and asserts that rights of each partner to satisfy his or her own desires, it is essential to recognize that healthy and wholesome physical nurturing puts the needs of the other first. The sexual part of a relationship is never to be about demanding something from each other.

Emotional nurturing is even more important than physical nurturing. Emotional nurturing depends on the willingness to communicate with mutual interests in mind.

One of the more important areas of emotional comfort centers on a couple's ability to communicate about their finances. However, this is not about how much money you have but rather how the family income is managed. Households with high-end incomes can still be plagued with insecurities and broken relationships. And homes with much less can still be content just because the use of those limited funds are not wasted or used selfishly or carelessly. Bills need to be paid, food needs to be put on the table, and couples need to work together to provide a safe home and a loving environment.

Traditionally, the husband carries the weight of providing financially – and more will be said about that in a coming chapter – but in today's economic environment, many times, both husband and wife have to work. When that happens, it is even more important than spending is a mutual plan. Often one income pays for house and utilities and major bills while the other covers the food and gas and clothes, for example. But no matter what the plan may be, each must respect the contribution that the other is making and never take that for granted.

No couple will agree on everything. Both spouses may have quite different opinions, but that does not mean they can't respect each other. Life is full of such matters as how to correct a child, in-law experiences, along with those truly pivotal issues of politics and paint colors, dogs vs. cats, and Coke vs. Pepsi. Every decision is an opportunity to strengthen each other's emotional lives simply by caring enough to put the other's needs and desires in perspective.

Marriage counselors often suggest that couples have an agreement on how much each one can spend on their own. If the income is small, they may want to set that figure as low as $20 for unplanned purchases. If an item costs more than the agreed amount, the couple can discuss it and decide whether the purchase is wise or necessary. This kind of relationship nurtures respect and interdependence that strengthens both spouses and helps make them feel loved and valued.

NURTURING – EMOTIONAL CARE

*O*f course, emotional support can take many forms, such as frequent hugs and kisses, offering to help each other with routine tasks, going out of your way to speak kindly about your in-laws, keeping any criticisms about each other to a minimum, and always wrapped in kindness and care, to name a few. Set aside a specific time as often as is needed to discuss any area of concern or disagreement. Talk to each other about your dreams or goals and be ready to ask the other what he or she needs from you to reach those goals.

Emotional needs may, at times, be immediate and life-changing. A loss of a parent or sibling, the loss of a job, children who are ill or are in trouble with authorities, a doctor's visit that reveals a significant threat to one's health, falling victim to some kind of violence – all are examples that require couples to provide extra support and comfort for each other. Each must strengthen the other.

And when there is a breakdown of the relationship and lack of trust causes an emotional low, act with genuine grace. No relationship fails because of the action of only one spouse. Healthy, nurturing relationships include an openness on each one's part to recognize your part of the problem. Admit your shortcomings and failures to be nurturing and loving, and always be ready to offer forgiveness for the failings of the other. Nothing will heal an emotional breach more than a loving and nurturing response that seeks to forgive and be forgiven.

Of course, there are many smaller ways to nurture your spouse and strengthen a sense of personal worth. Husbands, offer to help your wife make dinner. Just ask what you can do to help. You may even want to learn to cook. If cooking is not your strong suit, then assume the role of the dishwasher. When you see her dusting and sweeping, step in and give her a moment to rest. If one of you is tired, the other could sit down and gently rub their neck or back. A husband may want to realize that offering to comb his wife's hair has a unique value to her once in a while.

On the other hand, kisses and hugs or any shows of affection should not always be a prelude to sex. Such gestures should be a natural part of every day, but not a cue that either is demanding sex from the other. And a special word to the men: women sometimes need to feel loved and appreciated without always having to respond to a sexual expectation.

When all else is said and done, the nurturing experience is based on the commitment to value your spouse more than yourself.

But here again, it is that matter of self-value.

In one sense, nurturing another to grow and become stronger can be affected by how well you nurture yourself emotionally. Physically we take care of ourselves by practicing hygiene, exercising, eating well, and getting adequate sleep, but emotionally self-nurture is often neglected.

A major building block of developing a nurturing relationship is how you invest in your emotional growth.

Let's talk about us men first.

Every man has to grow up. Men can often be little boys in big bodies. Maturity is not about size but about putting the boyish life behind you and developing a sense of independence and responsibility.

When we become men, our priorities change. Our families and our jobs are more important than just hanging out with our buddies. Don't get me wrong here. Men need strong, healthy relationships with other men who are trustworthy and mature.

These will be men who share your values and model for you and others the same commitments you have in your life.

Women also need to have other women friends who see each other with the same lens. These will be wives and mothers who experience the same kind of struggles and hopes, dream the same dreams and carry the same type of loads. They can learn from each other and comfort each other.

Both men and women need the strength and nurturing growth that comes with healthy social support. Friends who have positive outlooks, similar hobbies, and interests can provide vital emotional support.

Nurturers are people who chose to focus on the needs of others.

Couples need to say "I love you" to each other every day, a purposeful practice that may not come as easily for a man as it does for a woman. We men must complement our wives on how they look, how they cook, or the way they decorate the home. We need to let them know that we notice what they achieve, especially things that are new to them or the changes they have made. That kind of attention comforts them and lets them know we do not take them for granted.

Women should realize that compliments build up their men. When wives acknowledge the things their husbands do around the house or help the family, they strengthen their spouses' desire to do more and become better than he already is.

Couples should listen and find out what each other's dreams are so they can help each other reach those goals. Imagine a relationship in which each spends more time pointing out each other's mistakes and shortcomings than focusing on the positives in each other. No relationship can grow without mutual attention to emotional support and nurturing.

Nurturing is a choice to be proactive. When things around the house are not being taken care of or not going well, the nurturer sets the tone that allows the family to come up with a way to solve problems without focusing on blame. When we have a family that needs our attention and help, we can't run and hide. Husbands, when you see your wives overwhelmed with responsibility, step in and help. Pick up a dishrag. Grab the vacuum or broom. Pick up toys or magazines or clothes or help with the pet. Children who see a parent modeling a nurturing role learn to become nurturers as well.

Every relationship will have misunderstandings, but we can't allow some problems to go unaddressed and worsen. Emotions may build up. Frustrations may become evident. We may need to let our emotions "cool off" to discuss the issue calmly and caringly. Such matters should never be allowed to lead to harsh or abusive language. Such reactions can, over time, too easily escalate to physical abuse that destroys the family.

Again, men often have problems knowing how to respond when their wives when emotions begin to build. A woman's emotions build up differently than in a man, so her husband must not overreact when she needs to vent.

Sometimes, she may need to have a few minutes by herself. If that is the case, her husband must not interpret that as a personal rejection. He needs to simply give her a hug or a kiss, say "I love you," and leave the room for a while. He may want to be the knight on the white horse coming to her rescue with solutions to the problem, but that only makes things worse while she is overwhelmed with her feelings.

Emotional nurturing at times like these has to be focused on her immediate need to be loved and comforted. She needs to know how important she is to her husband. And her husband needs to practice listening. When she wants to talk, he needs to be attentive and learn what she really needs. He should discover her limits so he can help avoid the kind of situations that trigger those limits.

The purpose of the nurturer is to maintain peace and order in the home. The solution to any conflict in a family is for both parties to win. Pause before speaking. Conflicts arise when we say things that hurt each other. We should be slow to get angry with everyone in our realm of influence. We need to know the facts and not jump to conclusions. The nurturer's goal is to handle all matters for the good of the whole family,

Disagreements and even arguments should be handled calmly when there are children present. Seeing anger and hearing ugly things being said between their parents can be very devastating to the way children grow up to treat others. Arguments that turn into fighting don't bring people together in the home. It pulls them apart.

Emotional nurturing is also protective. Every family experiences change, but we must take care that change is not forced on us by others. Even with all its pressures and problems, our job must not be allowed to cause any unwanted change in our relationships. At times our extended families may try to change us. Parents or other relatives, even former spouses, may try to influence us to change. Changes made without the family making the best decisions for them will become hindrances to our emotional health and stability.

There are so many things that can interrupt our relationships and damage them, and in the end, our desires to be emotionally strong can only take us so far. Our lives had to have a firm foundation stronger than we are.

The third area of care is spiritual. This is by far the greatest need in any relationship, yet it may be the most neglected.

NURTURING – SPIRITUAL CARE

*H*ave you ever seen a three-legged stool?

It takes no real imagination to figure out what happens when one of those legs is missing. You might be able to balance yourself for a moment, but in the end, that's just where you'll land, on your end.

We have looked at physical nurturing and what that means.

We should make sure we eat right, and our family eats right. We should make sure our kids get a good education by getting to know the teachers, watching what our kids are being taught, and checking homework. We are to provide our family with a good home to live in and see that their health needs are met.

We must continue to grow by educating ourselves and pass the knowledge we have received on to our spouses and children. We must motivate each other to grow and be productive.

We need to model good hygiene, take care of our appearance. Physical nurturing includes such everyday things like combing our hair, taking care of our clothes, and basic cleanliness.

Men, in particular, need to set the tone in their family for personal care. Failure to do this regularly will cause others to lose respect for you and your family. Men who respect others also respect themselves and model that for their families. Set the pace, be the example, and your family will more likely follow in your steps.

We have also looked at emotional nurturing.

The physical care we give ourselves produces good emotional care for the family as well. We have looked at our need to handle difficulties with strength and wisdom that puts the family first. We bring the family together to own the problems and solve them together. Our actions invest each family member, beginning with our spouses, with a strong sense of being loved, valued, and ultimately safe.

We have to look at how to resolve problems and conflict to avoid blame and enjoy mutual respect. As nurturers, we seek to protect the family. Jobs and other outside influences must never interfere with the peace and oneness of the family.

But now, we turn our attention to the most

important nurturing of all: the spiritual care of our spouses and children.

The example of the three-legged stool loses some meaning here since all three legs of the stool are of equal importance. The point is that the other two by themselves are not enough. But there, the illustration ends.

Spiritual nurturing is more like the foundation of your house. If the foundation is not laid correctly, the house will not stand.

In the same way, if the spiritual foundation of your home is not solid and well-tended, the relationships in the home will be unstable; and if they last, they will be unhealthy and potentially toxic.

All of our lives and relationships have the potential for greatness in a variety of ways. But the basis for any growth or achievement we experience needs to be built on our willingness to allow God to direct us and be pleased with how we live our lives. Our ability to manage our homes, families, careers and the relationships He allows us to have must have the foundation of His love and care, His nurturing presence in our own lives. Life under His nurturing hands can be blessed with strength and growth, and as God chooses, even more dreams and responsibilities.

If you are reading this book, you are the kind of man or woman who wants to have healthy, happy, and loving relationships. You want or have a view of life in which you want to influence and make a difference in the world positively. You want to maintain your responsibility to honor your parents, love your spouse and children. You want to be there for them and support and nurture them.

Yet you already know that your best efforts are not enough. You try but often fall short of your hopes. The missing piece to this puzzle of life is the spiritual nurturing you need to help others be spiritually healthy.

If you genuinely want the paths and circumstances of life to be better, you must look to the One who gave you life and loves you enough to nurture you. Each of us must place our faith in God and, with His hand leading us, take control of our lives by giving that control to Him.

Remember our earlier discussion about basics? That's where we are going to start.

The question underlying everything in this book is, "What is love?" All our talk of healthy growing relationships and areas of nurturing have one common factor: love. So, we need to be clear about what love is and what it is not.

I looked up the word *love* in a popular dictionary. It was defined as follows:

(a) strong affection for another arising out

of kinship or personal ties (maternal-
for a child).
(b) attraction based on sexual desire:
affection and tenderness, felt by lovers.

Those two short statements sum up the common view of love in society today. But sadly, they are inadequate.

Then I looked up *love* in the Bible, where we discover that God has given us a vastly different perspective of love. In fact, in 1 John 4:8, we read, "God is love." It does not simply say that God loves, but that Love is who He is. Love is embodied in Him.

All through the Bible, God tells us about love. He reveals Himself page after page, chapter after chapter, because the more we discover about God, the more we can know about love. In fact, if we don't know Him, we haven't discovered love as God intended for us to experience.

Here are just a few of the many things God's word tell us about real and pure love:

Love is measured by the way Christ loves
us (Jn. 15: 12).
Loving others is also measured by how one
loves himself (Mt. 22: 39).
Love is a gift given to us by the Holy Spirit
(2 Cor. 6: 6).

> *Loving involves the heart, soul, mind and strength (Mt. 22: 37; Lk. 10: 27).*
> *Love makes us willing to lay down our own lives for others (Jn. 15: 13).*
> *Love is demonstrated by our service to others (Gal. 5: 13).*
> *Love has no place for fear (John 4:18).*
> *Love has no place for hypocrisy (Romans 12:9).*
> *Love has no place for insincerity (2 Corinthians 8:8).*

And if you want to know why this book has its title, look at what 1 Jn. 3:18 has to say:

> *Let's not merely say that we love each other; let us show the truth by our actions.*

Love is more than just a word, but something we do. Love causes us to act on it. In other words: Love is an Action!

We throw the word *love* around today so freely; and, in truth, carelessly.

Genuine love must be shown. Others must experience love if the words are to have any real meaning. Just as God, who is Love personified, has shown His love to us, our declaration of love has to be evidenced in what we do. Our actions say what our words cannot.

To nurture spiritually is to be the instrument through whom God's love is introduced and experienced by those He has put in your life. The words "God loves you" mean very little if the one who says them does not act in a way that lets others experience that love.

In the relationships of a husband and wife or with other family members, love must reflect through you how God feels about those in your life. When disrespect and deceit are present, *love* is an empty word. If you are not truthful, if you are unfaithful and betraying your spouse's trust, your actions make the word *love* meaningless.

Those who choose to become spiritual nurturers may know the pain of rejection or any lack of love from another, but they have both the capability and the desire to good for evil, love for hatefulness. But be wise and seek the advice of a pastor, parents, good friends, and most of all, God Himself. With such understanding, you have a better chance of knowing how to love another without allowing them to harm or abuse you further.

The Bible tells us to forgive and forget. But we must avoid allowing people to continue hurting us, even if it means that the person can no longer be close to us again.

Two good things come from relationships; we mature and become very wise.

We learn about ourselves and the people close to

us, including the good, the positive, and the far less desirable side of our humanity. We experience loss and pain, sickness and loneliness, sometimes in others around us, and often in our own lives as well.

We also discover love when someone is there to listen in the middle of the night. We learn that love can be shared with a simple bowl of chicken soup or timely words to encourage us. Love warms us when a spouse or a friend cooks our favorite dish or brings us an unexpected gift.

How soothing are our spouses' hugs or kisses? And how reassuring love is when we realize that all our frailties that no one else knows or sees do not deter our spouses' from coming to our sides. He or she knows both our good points and our weaknesses, has lived with our habits and shortcomings, knows our tendencies to be selfish and unwilling to change. Yet they are there for us, patient with us, but with a firm love that seeks to nurture us and help us to grow.

How unbearable our loneliness or lostness would be except for the love that stays close and lifts us with a nurturing that resists stepping away.

In that kind of relationship, we can experience a shift in our lives that give us insight, wisdom and teaches us how to nurture in return.

We as parents must love our children enough that we correct them. Our love calls us to explain right and wrong to them, help them learn self-respect, and respect and value others. And most of all, they know how loved they are by the love their parents model for them.

Spiritual nurturing highlights the cause of all love and meaningfulness that brings the family relationship into balance.

NURTURING LOVE CANNOT WAIT

*G*od's nurturing care fills every day of our lives. There are not enough pages in all the books ever written to fully describe the love of God.

His desire to love us is not a mystery. After all, He made us in His own image. He loves us so much that when sin spoiled His creation and left us with a broken relationship with Him, He gave us His Son Jesus, who in turn gave Himself to be our Redeemer on the cross. We are restored to a relationship with God when we accept His Lordship over our lives.

God longs to have a loving and nurturing relationship with us.

This relationship begins when we receive Him as Lord of our lives. His word feeds us and nurtures us, so we can be strong and enjoy our walk with Him. He leads us to be part of a nurturing spiritual environment where a pastor and other Christians can set examples of living a life based on His guidelines, which is good for us and our neighbors.

Each day of our lives is filled with His blessings. The Bible tells us that all good things come from His hands (James 1:17). The sun He created provides us with light, and His night hours give us rest. The wonder of water that quenches our thirst and cleans our hands, and lets our plants grow is a miracle. We have minds and hearts that can know and grow and love.

And His blessings do not stop with this life. His love has prepared a place for us to enjoy being with Him forever.

Yet, even though we know that life is short and that someday we will die, we live day after day as if this life is all there is.

But the time for each of us is short and comes to an end. Life is full of time constraints, and time itself is the ultimate constraint.

His love nurtures us each of those days, and with His care, we are to nurture others while we can lovingly. We should do our best to demonstrate love to others every day, just as it is demonstrated to us. This will include family, friends, co-workers, church members, and anyone God entrusts with us. Undoubtedly, they will let you down in many different ways, and it may hurt. But God said in His word although others will let you down, He won't.

People will test our lives in the realm of our influence who will lie to us, betray us, steal from us, even attack or abuse us physically or emotionally. Some of our own children will hurt us when they refuse to listen to sound wisdom and turn against us. Some may give us great pain when they turn to a life of crime.

We must do what we can to help the people in our lives become what God intended them to be. We must never lose hope but always look to God for strength. When we feel our love is being pulled and tested like never before, God will help us stand strong.

As we help others, God will help us with the issues in our lives.

We must ready to forgive others as soon as we realize that our pain has turned to bitterness. God's love must be allowed to flow through us. As we pray, God will hear and answer us. It is possible to love the hell out of people.

We must be very wise and maintain order in our homes and teach respect for all mankind to our families. We must seek help from God, our Pastors, and other Godly men and women to help us if we are in any situation that leaves us uncertain or vulnerable, especially if we feel we are losing control.

Sometimes, we may think it's best to simply roll over, tuck ourselves away and "play dead," but we should not give in to that impulse. That is an act of neglect rather than love.

God can help us be people who will strengthen the family structure and be a positive example, bringing positive change all around us.

We all have something of value that can help somebody else. Let's not be selfish with it.

We need to love people even when they won't love us back at first. In time those we love will be affected by our love. After all, Jesus loves us before we were capable of loving Him in return.

We must never forget that we live in a dying world, and the people around us need to discover more than the fleshly version of love that the culture has to offer. Many of them are trapped in lives of abuse and neglect. They wear the scars of injustice and pain, often lashing out because of that pain.

Sometimes merely a kind word or a hug gives them a moment of relief. We may never even know when a helping hand in a time of need or a smile that says "I love you" will literally save someone's life. A genuine act of caring given with love and wisdom could turn someone around.

God calls us to be like Christ, who became a servant for us. When we serve others, supporting and encouraging them, we build them up. And those who have been loved will want to love and encourage others people as well.

Love, on the other hand, is an action word. The

kind of love that truly nurtures others is an act, something we do not just say. True love is missing in so many people's lives, and when an act of selflessness and humility touches them, they are introduced to the love of God through us.

Our world's moral fiber is becoming polluted and warped by a sense of love that is weak and temporary at best. The world has chosen to live outside of the boundaries God lovingly put in place to enjoy a healthy life with others around us.

His design declares how important we are to Him. It tells us that we have a part to play in God's divine plan. When we choose to live in His plan, we can truly impact others in our lives with light and life that is not constrained by the timeline of this world.

His love in us allows us to love and value others and realize that they are irreplaceable. Our time in this life is limited, and our calendars are always full, but we need to commit to spending time with those God has given us. Let us bring a positive light to their world.

Indeed, we can all agree that time is valuable, but we can also agree that while we may manage our time, we can't control the pace of life or what a day or an hour may bring.

That is why love can't wait. If we are not managing our time, we are losing it, and with each lost moment, an opportunity to love and care is lost.

That is especially important regarding our nurturing relationships in our immediate families.

Making good use of your time is essential in every aspect of life. When we graduate high school, we are supposed to have used that time to complete a 12th-grade education. There comes a time when we are expected to drive a car and have a little more independence. Time in our lives gets invested along with money and other resources in planning building projects, managing businesses, or running programs. Time is valuable to people who want to be more effective in relationships in every area of the workforce.

Time is needed to be healthy, exercise, and diet properly, all of which help you get proper rest. When time is invested in our personal care, we are more effective in our time management.

A wise person uses time wisely.

How often has valuable time been lost in your home life? Communication breaks down with your spouse or children. The television and our "right" to have some downtime after work sends others away. Any number of legitimate tasks of our day can create barriers with family members.

Many fathers struggle later in life to recall memories of these children growing up, but they can remember details about the job or the nights out with the guys. Parents can so easily miss valuable moments of their children growing up into young adulthood. What's sad is that if we neglect our children, others like a babysitter, their peers, the neighborhood drug dealers or gangs will influence them and instill core values in their minds. When we do get around them, we will wonder who taught them the negative behaviors they display.

When we make time for the people we love, we began to understand how they think and avoid confusion and misunderstandings. On the other hand, when we fail to make time for our kids and their school grades, some could eventually drop out of school. Their lives lack positive role models and self-esteem when loving, healthy nurturing is not in place.

We must show interest in the things our spouses and children are doing and the activities they are involved in if we are to hold the family together. The media promotes sex and violence all day long on many different levels that serve only to distract us from what is important around us and those we love.

Family values that once were promoted by society, in general, have been replaced by smut, vulgarity, and moral decline. If high moral values are not taught in the home and reinforced by the words of God and the spiritual nurturing of the parents, our children may never find the absolute love of a caring God.

When we spend time with our families, we

discover our strengths and weaknesses because our family will help make us aware of who we really are. Sometimes they tell us what they see in us, and other times we know because we see our values being modeled in them.

That's why we need to come home from work at a reasonable hour. We should find every member of the house and give them a few minutes of our time. This will let them know that they are important to you. And based on their behavior and how they respond to you with eye contact and the words they speak, you can gauge if they need more time with you.

We can learn life lessons from the oldest to the youngest family member if we spend time with them. I know most of us have busy lives, but we could lose the most important people in our lives simply because we are too busy trying to make a better life for them. Be assured that they would rather have more from you than your livelihood.

Those who choose to be healthy nurturers avoid any form of drugs and alcohol.

Such substances are forms of escape that produce only weakness and destruction in the family. They lead to downward spirals that steal your health and leave you with hopelessness instead. The loss of hope is a significant cause of suicide among both parents and children.

Families that nurture each other can face the

inevitable pains of life. Death, sickness, and disease come uninvited into your life. Job loss, disability, and homelessness can intrude from time to time. Rape, betrayal, hate, sorrow, grief, sadness, confusion, disappointment, discouragement, loss, along with injustice, may force their way into your family. But the family that has a loving, nurturing bond can survive. With the help of God and those who make time for us, the family's love and values make them strong.

Suffering will undoubtedly come to all of us. Families of every kind have issues in their lives.

And when tough times come, God's nurturing care can use them to help us grow and develop into the kinds of people He wants us to be.

LET'S GET PRACTICAL: RELATIONSHIP NOTES AND NUDGES

BEWARE OF PEOPLE WHO COULD
SABOTAGE YOUR LIFE

*B*e warned: some people can do more harm than good to a relationship.

Men and women who plan to have a life together need to be alert to specific behaviors that should send up red flags. Some of these behaviors may be evident early in the relationship. If so, run for your life! Or, they may show up later, even after you have been married for some time. You will want to try to work through them, and sometimes you can see progress, but you must realize that we can't change another adult unless they want to change. We can encourage it, but the decision is up to that individual.

NEGATIVE BEHAVIORS IN MEN

1) He can't keep his word.
Ladies, don't waste your time with a man who
doesn't keep his word, who isn't where he says he
will be, and doesn't do what he says he will do. Trust
can't be built on deception and lies.

2) He still lives with his parents.
If he has not learned to be on his own, avoid him. He
is likely too immature to know how to care for a
woman. Any relationship will be further strained by
the presence of his parents in matters that belong to
a couple themselves. A wife must be the most
important person in a man's life, not his parents.

3) He can't hold a job.
Money may not be the most important factor in a
relationship, but is it a major one. Life is demanding
without a steady income. While it is true that we
change jobs sometimes to have a better place to
work or make more money or have better benefits,
the man who can't hold a job usually is lazy or hard
to get along with and often doesn't appreciate the
value of work.

4) He is a con artist.
Ladies, run for your lives. Change your phone

number, and if you have known him for a while, change banks too. This kind of man uses people, even preys on them. He may appear like he has money and influence. He plays on your emotions, but all he wants is your money. When your money runs out, so will he.

.

5) He uses drugs and alcohol.
A man who uses these drugs or alcohol is likely to be an addict or become one, and he will take you on an emotional roller coaster as he struggles with his problem. His addictions will always be more important than you. Far too often, he will display abusive behavior toward his family members. Money matters in the home will be neglected because he will use money that should buy food, clothes, medication, and other bills to feed his addiction.

6) He has commitment issues.
Some men seem to resistant the idea of commitment, yet they want women to commit to them. At the same time, they keep playing the field. Move on.

7) He takes you for granted.
This kind of man is always too busy to spend any quality time with you. He fails to pay attention to

you, compliment you on new hairdos or new outfits. He has little if any interest in your accomplishments. He may love his job or even his ministry too much. He may prefer to spend time with his buddies. Or, he may even have another relationship on the side.

8) He thinks intimacy is only about sex.
Use the same rules you need if you catch fire. Stop, drop and roll. Stop seeing him, drop him like a hot rock, and roll on down the road. And be warned: these kinds of men are everywhere, even in the church.

9) He doesn't control his temper.
A man with an anger problem is a danger to you and any children in the family. Physical abuse is a serious danger, and emotional abuse can be just as severe, if not more so. Any abusive language that he uses toward you is a signal to leave.

10) He has no ambition.
A man who has no sense of direction, no dreams or ambition for him or you will accomplish very little. This kind of man has no sense of personal honor or self-respect.

NEGATIVE BEHAVIORS IN WOMEN

1) She is always loud and in the middle of confusion.
A woman who is boisterous and confusion seems to be a regular part of her social activities is self-centered and probably argumentative and divisive.

2) She dresses and acts provocatively.
This kind of woman has a weak sense of shame or, at times, no shame at all. Her choice to be provocative indicates a moral problem either from ignorance or a choice to be depraved. This is a temptress who preys on men and treats them as victims. She will come in different colors and sizes and may be rich or poor, but she is sexually manipulative and controlling.

3) She is lazy.
A woman who fails to keep herself clean and presentable will treat her home the same way. Her attitude will sabotage a relationship.

4) She can't manage money.
If a woman is unwilling to manage money wisely, she probably has no sense of what it takes to earn those dollars. Her priorities are based on satisfying

her whims, and she will have problems sharing family financial plans for controlling spending.

5) She can't get along with others.
Again, this woman is selfish and wants things her way. Relationships are focused only on her.
.

6) She is a "silly" woman.
Silly or naïve people are easily led astray, even seduced emotionally or physically. This is a woman who will struggle to be faithful to you or anyone else.

7) She is inflexibly stubborn.
Like the woman who can't get along with others, an inflexible woman will refuse to place any value on what others think. She will resist anyone who tries to exercise any leadership over her.

8) She wants to hang out with her friends all the time.
This is another sign of selfishness that makes it very difficult for us to care about the needs of others.

Let me add that there is no perfect man or woman, but the guidelines above should help us recognize a potential relationship barrier. And these traits should cause us to look at our behaviors and choices, so we will not be toxic to potential relationships.

THOUGHTS ABOUT SEX

$\mathcal{I}$f we believe that God is our ultimate Source of love; and that as our Creator, He has designed us to function perfectly as He planned, then every aspect of our lives should reflect His purposes and plans. That would certainly include the subject of sex.

Why did God create us to be sexual beings?

I believe God's intentions for sex are much different than what our society has made it out to be. Primarily God's plan for sex is to allow us to reproduce. He designed men and women differently and compatibly. Sex is a function to be used in the sacred bond of marriage. And, let's be clear, if he did not want the husband and the wife to enjoy sex, he would not have added that into the formula.

Sex is to be respected as His provision, yet the world has defiled this sacred part of our nature. Sex without the commitment of marriage is now the accepted norm. Pornography is no longer sold in dark alleys. Abortion is a national shame. The growing number of rapes and abuse is alarming. The merchandising industry adds to the distortion by its mantra "sex sells." Prostitution and various forms of sex trafficking have turned women and men, girls and boys, into slaves whose lives and family lives are damaged, sometimes beyond repair.

Even among married couples, the motivation to have more and more children seems driven by how much money the government will give you. The sacredness of a child is lost in the greediness of custody battles and the dickering over child support.

Married couples who understand that mutual submission in the bond of marriage and allows them to care for each other's needs should make their sexual lives meet that expectation. Sex isn't a perfect ten every time for either partner, but you can make it your goal to please your spouse even more than yourself.

Don't treat sex as a routine or simply a demand made by one on the other. Marriage is a loving and nurturing relationship, and sex is one of the ways God has designed for us to do that. Tenderness, before and after intercourse, is an integral part of sex.

Just one added thought. Sex education belongs to the parents. Schools are teaching our children at almost every grade level about sex. They tell our kids that sex is okay as long as they have protection. Our kids are exposed to an increasing number of sexual issues that are being raised today.

The subject of sex, as should be the case with everything else about life, should be heard first from mom and dad.

WARNINGS ABOUT MONEY

*W*hile money was discussed in an earlier chapter, here are some added thoughts to say that money is a good thing to have if kept in the proper perspective.

We want better lifestyles, homes, cars, and vacations. We want our kids to have good educations.

But we have to be careful about what we want. If our desires are not healthy, our money will be wasted on entertainment instead of clothing, on drugs instead of paying bills, on sex and favors to feed our greed, instead of feeding our families.

Refuse to be governed by greed. Greed will alter your judgment and end up exploiting others rather than helping them.

Seek God's direction to be generous. Others need our help. Those living in inner cities or those living in faraway places need our help. Churches, schools, medical facilities, playgrounds, parks, streets, and buildings can benefit from the gifts of our money. Single moms, young people who are being dragged into crime, the wildlife preserves, or neighborhood clinics all need our help.

Generous people help our world become a better place.

AND THEN THERE IS "THE STUFF"

And then there is "the stuff"

WHAT IS "THE STUFF?"

That would be cars, homes, clothes, shoes, jewelry, the latest gadgets and phones, and electronics, clothes, toys for big boys and girls, and more clothes, toys for men, and more.

You've heard about keeping up with the Joneses, haven't you? Well, the truth is that in many cases, the Joneses are only broke at a higher level than you are.

Living for "the stuff" feeds your greed and whets your debt.

Debt kills. Sometimes literally. The stress of debt can lead to illness and even death. Then other people get to enjoy or abuse all "the stuff" you collected.

Keep "the stuff" in perspective. Remember that you and your resources belong to God and let Him have first place in your life.

ABOUT THE AUTHOR

Pastors Kurt and Janice Broadnax are the Pastor and wife of Bread of Life Church. They served as Founders of Bread of Life Church in Killeen, Texas. Our first service was on August 6, 2017, in Copperas Cove, Texas. We then relocated to Killeen, Texas. We held our first service on April 1, 2018, at our present location, 2300 East Rancier Suite 108, Killeen, Texas 76543.

Pastor Kurt serves as the Senior Pastor of Bread of Life Church - Killeen, Texas. His leadership experiences include serving in numerous positions within the church and non-profit organizations, 15 years of military service as an enlisted soldier and non-commissioned officer, and ten years as a veteran service representative.

His education accomplishments include Associate degrees in Air Conditioning and General Studies at Central Texas College Killeen, Texas, Completed School of ministry TD Igerhart, Texas Southwest Church of God in Christ.

Lady Janice serves as the Women Department Leader, and she supports her husband in the church's daily operation. Lady Janice earned her Associate's Degree in Nursing from The Temple College, Temple Texas, and has worked in nursing for over 25 years.

They have resided in Killeen, Texas, since 2000.

Happily married for 27 years, they have no biological children. However, they are recognized as Godparents.

Pastor Kurt and Lady Janice are committed to God and connected to their spiritual leadership in the Church of God in Christ denomination.

LOVE FOR GOD

Pastor Kurt and Lady Janice's obedience to God is demonstrated in their commitment to Him, one another, their family, and all of God's children. Their time spent with Him is reflected in their conduct and character wherever you may encounter them.

LOVE FOR ONE ANOTHER

As heirs of the grace of life together, Pastor Kurt and Janice embrace the uniqueness of who God has designed each of them to be, yet celebrating the oneness that they have as husband and wife. When God restored their marriage, they are committed to challenging husbands and wives to submit to God's will, word and way.

LOVE FOR FAMILY

Pastor Kurt and Lady Janice enjoy spending time with one another and their extended family in Killeen, Texas.

LOVE FOR GOD'S PEOPLE

It is the preeminence of God in their lives that drives Pastor Kurt and Lady Janice to share the faithfulness of God with anyone willing to listen. Their testimony is that the God who saved, delivered, and restored their marriage and family can do the same for anyone willing to call upon and surrender to Him completely.

 facebook.com/kurt.broadnax

 twitter.com/ktbdx

 instagram.com/kurtjanice

linkedin.com/in/kurt-broadnax-08110a20

CPSIA information can be obtained
at www.ICGtesting.com
Printed in the USA
BVHW041706080721
611459BV00015B/1104